Queens of Capital Collective Publishing

From Failure to Fortune: The Daily Affirmation Journal

Because every Queen has a chapter she doesn't brag about… but that chapter built her crown.

Cortlandt Coleman

Copyright

Dedication: The Final Crown

To my children,

Kailie, Katelandt, and Kody Davis.

You are the heartbeat behind my purpose and the light that guides every step I

take.

Everything I do, I do with you in mind.

Every lesson I learn, every battle I fight, every victory I claim.

I carry each of you with me.

May this book remind you that strength can be born from struggle, purpose can

rise from pain, and greatness lives within your name.

I love you more than words will ever hold.

"Everything I endured was preparation.
Everything I learned became protection.
And everything I built was for the legacy that follows me."

Acknowledgement

First, I thank God, the Author of my life, for every lesson that shaped me into the woman I am today. Every season carried a purpose. Every encounter taught me something I needed to hold, release, or grow from. His timing, His pruning, and His positioning aligned me with every woman and man who crossed my path in divine order, all contributing to the Queen I am becoming.

To my husband, our twenty-year journey has taught me that storms are necessary for growth. The greatest lessons are learned at home, not on the streets. Thank you for being imperfect in ways that strengthened me, for teaching me boundaries, coping skills, and money management, and for loving me through every season. Even when I showed up with fire, passion, and a strong spirit.

To my children and bonus children, thank you for allowing me to be your mother, even when my venting sessions turned into life documentaries meant to guide, protect, and prepare you. You are my purpose in motion. Watching you grow has stretched me, humbled me, and strengthened my walk in ways I never imagined.

To my mother and grandmother, you shaped my foundation. Your strength, wisdom, discipline, and resilience live within me every day.

To my father, thank you for consistently pushing me to be better and do better. Your influence is woven into my ambition, my discipline, and my drive to rise higher.

To my grandchildren, thank you for restoring youth, joy, and life within my spirit. You remind me daily why legacy matters.

To every person who encountered me in any season, whether I was broken or healed, thank you. Each of you played a role in molding the leader, woman, and Queen I stand as today.

To my mentors, Joseph and Malisha Ward, thank you for shaping me, stretching me, and molding me into greatness. Your guidance, leadership, and belief in my potential gave me the courage to evolve, elevate, and sharpen my vision.

And to my little sister, you are the light of my existence. Being the first daughter and grandchild created a deep sense of responsibility, protection, and purpose within me for you and our family. Thank you for introducing me to Justin and Portia Johnson, whose influence opened the door to the financial services industry that transformed my life. That introduction became the foundation of my purpose, my calling, and ultimately, this journal.

To every Queen holding this book, thank you for allowing me to pour my story into your healing, your elevation, and you're becoming. May these pages remind you that nothing you experienced was wasted. Every lesson, every tear, and every triumph helped shape your crown.

— *Cortlandt Coleman*

Table of Content

Reflections of a Queen

A final space for journaling, prayer, and gratitude.

Author's Introduction

"Discipline births power. Mindset builds legacy."

See, it was always a dream of mine to write something that could *inspire other Queens* not just to be good, but to **become great.**

To align their thoughts, sharpen their mindsets, and shift their perspective toward abundance, especially financial abundance.

Because a disciplined Queen is a *dangerous Queen.*

She can jump through hoops, move mountains, and still fix her crown before anyone notices the sweat.

She learns to control her environment, master her emotions, and execute with grace even when life tests her strength.

But I had to learn that kind of power didn't come easy.

It came from self-awareness, structure, and surrender.

It came from realizing that my thoughts were shaping my reality and that if I wanted a better life, I had to start by thinking better.

When that truth hit me, I picked up my Bible.

Then I started reading books that forced me to look inward to address the internal battles silently controlling my success.

See, success isn't about perfection.

It's about **mastering yourself, your focus, and your flaws.**

For me, that mastery started with something simple at one time.

I used to be late to everything, and honestly, I didn't care.

But when I learned that *being early means being prepared*, I crushed a poor mindset that had been costing me opportunities.

It wasn't just about showing up; it was about **showing up ready.**

So, this journal was born out of discipline, growth, and transformation.
It's for every woman who's tired of surviving and ready to *become.*
For the Queens ready to rewrite their stories, align their habits with heaven, and walk boldly in purpose, wealth, and wisdom.

I pray this journal ignites that fire in you, the one that reminds you that greatness isn't out there somewhere.
It's already *in you.*
Now it's time to water it.

"My Breaking Point Became My Blueprint."

Since I was a child, I've known what it feels like to be in an absent love.
My father served our country, and although I knew he loved me, his career kept him far away from home, on long tours, and with very little communication. His absence left an open space where masculine love, wisdom, and affirmation should've been.

I was raised by my mother and grandmother, two powerful Black women who embodied strength, resilience, and faith. My mother taught me grace: to be kind, gentle, and well-presented, to know my worth, and never to compromise my values for a man. My grandmother taught me grit: the laws of the streets, how to be a boss, and how to move in silence, never letting anyone know the difference between my left hand and my right.

But even with their guidance, something was missing. See, a father's role goes beyond the provision he gives a daughter safety, validation, and a model of how a man *should* protect, love, and lead. My mother and grandmother could teach me how to navigate men, but they couldn't teach me how a man thinks.

So when I met my first boyfriend, a few years older, attentive, and full of charm, I felt something I had longed for: security, love, and acceptance. He believed in my dreams and listened when I spoke. It was my first experience of feeling emotionally covered. But after three years, life took us in different directions. He was in college, and I had just graduated. When he ended things, I was shattered.

That heartbreak awakened something more profound, a longing to fill the void I had carried since childhood. I began searching for what I had lost, not realizing I was chasing something only God could restore.

Then I met the man who would become my husband. The relationship took off fast, love, passion, and soon after, a baby. But along with that came reality: he was facing legal trouble, and I was facing motherhood. I remember thinking, *What have I gotten myself into?* I was scared, pregnant, and staring at a future that didn't look like the one I dreamed of.

When he served sixteen months in jail, that season became my breaking point but also my awakening. My loyalty told me to stand by him, and my upbringing told me never to abandon someone in their lowest moment. But deep down, I realized God was forcing me to shift my focus from trying to fix others to developing *myself.*

That journey through heartbreak, betrayal, and uncertainty was the beginning of my transformation. I went back to school, earned my degree in Healthcare Management, and found purpose in helping others. But soon, I realized I was still serving, just not in the area that changed lives long-term. That's when I pivoted into **financial services** to teach low-income and middle-class families how to break cycles of debt, paycheck-to-paycheck living, and economic dependency.

I went from collecting payments to creating pathways from helping people survive to teaching them how to **build wealth, stability, and legacy.**

This *right here* was my break. My pain became purpose. My mistakes became my message. My breaking point became my blueprint.

Author Signature

With Love, Power & Purpose,

Cortlandt Coleman

Founder, Queens of Capital Collective

Creator of the Queens of Capital Collective 90-day Planner

Author *of From Failure to Fortune: The Daily Affirmation Journal*

"Discipline your mind, protect your peace, and the crown will follow."

Day 1 — The Root: Purpose in the Pain

"Every hardship that once broke me was really preparing me to rebuild stronger."

My Reflection

There was a time when I thought pain meant punishment; that every heartbreak, setback, and closed door was a sign that I wasn't enough.
But what I later learned is this: **pain is the invitation to transformation.**

If life had stayed comfortable, I never would've developed the strength to stand tall.
If everything had gone my way, I never would've discovered what I was made of.

Your pain is not your ending, it's your enrollment into purpose.
Every lesson, loss, and late-night shapes the woman you are becoming.

Today's Affirmation

"I no longer run from my pain. I face it, learn from it, and allow it to push me toward my purpose."

Journal Prompt

- What moment in your life felt like a breaking point, but later revealed itself as a blessing in disguise?

- What did that season teach you about your strength and resilience?

- How can you use that same energy to push forward today?

Note to Self

You've survived every challenging thing you thought would destroy you; that means you are already equipped to build the life you desire.

Reflections of a Queen

"Pause. Reflect. Realign."

Take a moment to breathe and let today's lesson settle in your spirit.
Use this space to write your thoughts, emotions, or next steps.
There's no right or wrong way to reflect, only honesty and intention.

What I Learned Today:

(What truth stood out the most to you from today's message?)

____

____

____

____

How I Feel Right Now:

(How did this chapter shift your emotions, mindset, or motivation?)

____

____

____

____

How I'll Apply It:

(What action, boundary, or habit will you commit to changing or improving after reading this?)

____

____

____

____

Prayer or Affirmation for Today:

(Write a short prayer or affirmation that aligns with what you're learning and becoming.)

____

____

____

____

"Discipline your mind, protect your peace, and the crown will follow."
— *Cortlandt Coleman*

"Out of difficulties grow miracles."

—Jean de La Bruyère

Day 2 — Breaking the Cycle: Healing the Inner Girl

"The little girl in me just wanted to feel seen, safe, and chosen. Today, I choose her."

My Reflection

There was a time when I didn't realize how much my childhood shaped the woman I became. The girl who felt unseen by her father became the woman searching for validation in others.
The girl who wanted to feel protected became the woman who tried to protect everyone else, even at the cost of her peace.

But healing isn't about blaming where you came from; it's about understanding what shaped you and choosing not to repeat the same cycle.

When I finally looked at that little girl in the mirror, I told her, *"You are not forgotten. You are not hard to love. You are worthy of everything you desire."*
And that's when the healing started.

You can't build wealth, peace, or legacy from a wounded foundation. Healing your inner child is how you pay off emotional debt before you pay off financial debt.

Today's Affirmation

"I honor the little girl within me. I give her safety, love, and permission to rest. I am no longer chasing what I already carry within."

Journal Prompt

- What did your younger self need to hear that she never did?

- How can you speak to that little girl today with compassion instead of criticism?

- What habits, beliefs, or people do you need to release to protect her peace?

Note to Self

Every healed piece of you becomes a stronger piece of your legacy. The more you love your inner child, the more powerful your future Queen becomes.

Reflections of a Queen

"Pause. Reflect. Realign."

Take a moment to breathe and let today's lesson settle in your spirit.
Use this space to write your thoughts, emotions, or next steps.
There's no right or wrong way to reflect, only honesty and intention.

What I Learned Today:

(What truth stood out the most to you from today's message?)

____

____

____

____

How I Feel Right Now:

(How did this chapter shift your emotions, mindset, or motivation?)

____

____

____

____

How I'll Apply It:

(What action, boundary, or habit will you commit to changing or improving after reading this?)

____

____

____

____

Prayer or Affirmation for Today:

(Write a short prayer or affirmation that aligns with what you're learning and becoming.)

____

____

____

____

"Discipline your mind, protect your peace, and the crown will follow."
— *Cortlandt Coleman*

"You are never too old to set another goal or to dream a new dream."

— C.S. Lewis

Day 3 — Forgive, But Don't Forget the Lesson

"God will use pain to open your eyes, but peace comes when you finally stop reopening the wound."

My Reflection

Forgiveness isn't easy, especially when you gave your best to people who didn't see your worth.

For a long time, I carried resentment. I replayed every conversation, every betrayal, every moment I wished I had handled differently.

Then one day, I realized: **holding on was holding me back.**

Forgiveness didn't mean pretending it didn't happen. It meant releasing my right to replay it. It meant saying, *"God, I trust You more than I trust my pain."*

Through every mistake, disappointment, and dark season, I learned that my **gut and my God were never wrong.**

Every time I ignored that small whisper inside, I paid for it emotionally, spiritually, or financially.

But every time I listened, even when it didn't make sense, peace followed.

Sometimes, forgiveness isn't for others. It's for the version of *you* who stayed too long, believed too much, or forgot your own power.

Today's Affirmation

"I release what hurt me, but I keep what taught me. I forgive fully, trust deeply, and follow the wisdom God placed inside me."

Journal Prompt

- Who or what do you still need to forgive to move forward?

- What lessons did that pain teach you about yourself or your boundaries?

- When was the last time your gut warned you, and how can you honor that inner voice, moving forward?

Note to Self

Peace doesn't come from forgetting. It comes from remembering wisely. Trust God, trust your intuition, that's the foundation of discernment and destiny.

Reflections of a Queen

"Pause. Reflect. Realign."

Take a moment to breathe and let today's lesson settle in your spirit. Use this space to write your thoughts, emotions, or next steps freely. There's no right or wrong way to reflect, only honesty and intention.

What I Learned Today:

(What truth stood out the most to you from today's message?)

How I Feel Right Now:

(How did this chapter shift your emotions, mindset, or motivation?)

____

____

____

____

How I'll Apply It:

(What action, boundary, or habit will you commit to changing or improving after reading this?)

____

____

____

____

Prayer or Affirmation for Today:

(Write a short prayer or affirmation that aligns with what you're learning and becoming.)

____

____

____

____

"Discipline your mind, protect your peace, and the crown will follow."
— *Cortlandt Coleman*

"Forgiveness does not change the past, but it does enlarge the future."

— Paul Boese

Day 4 — Becoming Her: The Woman I Prayed to Be

"I stopped praying for the life I wanted and started preparing for the woman who could handle it."

My Reflection

For years, I prayed for peace, stability, and purpose.
Now, standing here as a wife, mother of three, and grandmother, I can see that every season, even the painful ones, was shaping me into the woman I prayed to become.

The woman I am today didn't arrive overnight. She was built through sleepless nights, silent prayers, and quiet acts of faith. I used to think the goal was success, but I learned the goal was **becoming**.

I prayed for financial freedom, and God gave me lessons in discipline.
I prayed for strength, and He gave me situations that required it.
I prayed for peace, and He taught me to let go.

I learned that if you want to reach the top, you must first learn how to take care of the people at the bottom, the overlooked, the undervalued, and even the small responsibilities that test your character when no one is watching.

The woman I prayed to be is not just blessed, she's a blessing.
She moves with strategy, speaks with grace, and carries herself like the crown never fell off.
She's financially free, spiritually grounded, and emotionally rich.
She leads her home, her business, and her legacy with love and divine order.

Becoming *her* is not a destination; it's a daily decision to grow, give, and glow.

Today's Affirmation

"I am walking in alignment with the woman I prayed to be a wise, wealthy, and whole Queen who leads with purpose and peace."

Journal Prompt

- Who is the woman you've been praying to become, and how close are you to meeting her today?

- What "small things" are you tending to now that are preparing you for the next level?

- How can you use your wisdom to pour into your children, grandchildren, and community without losing yourself?

Note to Self

The woman you prayed to be is already inside you. Keep trusting God's timing, mastering the trivial things, and moving with grace; your life is the testimony now.

Reflections of a Queen

"Pause. Reflect. Realign."

Take a moment to breathe and let today's lesson settle in your spirit.
Use this space to write your thoughts, emotions, or next steps.
There's no right or wrong way to reflect, only honesty and intention.

What I Learned Today:

(What truth stood out the most to you from today's message?)

____

____

____

____

How I Feel Right Now:

(How did this chapter shift your emotions, mindset, or motivation?)

____

____

____

____

How I'll Apply It:

(What action, boundary, or habit will you commit to changing or improving after reading this?)

____

____

____

____

Prayer or Affirmation for Today:

(Write a short prayer or affirmation that aligns with what you're learning and becoming.)

____

____

____

____

"Discipline your mind, protect your peace, and the crown will follow."
— *Cortlandt Coleman*

"Be yourself; everyone else is already taken."

— Oscar Wilde

Day 5 — Moving in Silence: Power Without Proving

"Elevation requires isolation. When you quiet the noise, you can finally hear the instructions."

My Reflection

I used to want people to see my progress to prove that I was making moves, healing, and evolving.

But then I realized, *absolute power doesn't announce itself.*

When you start leveling up, it exposes everything around you, not just your potential, but people's intentions.

Some friends will clap for your success publicly but compete with you privately.

Others will admire your growth until it outgrows their comfort zone.

That's when God teaches you the beauty of moving in silence.

It's not about being secretive, it's about being **selective.**

Everyone doesn't deserve access to your next level, especially those who envy instead of evolving.

When you start purging your circle, you'll notice something sacred happens:

The ones who were draining your energy disappear, and the ones meant to align with your purpose start to appear.

That's not loss, that's *divine subtraction for abundance expansion.*

I've learned that the loudest person in the room usually has the least power.

The woman I am today moves strategically. I don't need to broadcast my every move; my results will speak louder than any post ever could.

Today's Affirmation

"I move in silence and let God make the noise. I attract divine connections and release those who no longer align with my purpose."

Journal Prompt

- Who in your current circle truly supports your growth, and who secretly competes with it?

- What boundaries do you need to set to protect your peace and progress?

- What does "moving in silence" look like for you emotionally, spiritually, and financially?

Note to Self

Don't explain your elevation. Protect your vision, guard your peace, and trust that God reveals the right people at the right time. When you release the enviousness, you make room for the abundant.

Reflections of a Queen

"Pause. Reflect. Realign."

Take a moment to breathe and let today's lesson settle in your spirit.
Use this space to write your thoughts, emotions, or next steps.
There's no right or wrong way to reflect, only honesty and intention.

What I Learned Today:

(What truth stood out the most to you from today's message?)

____

____

____

____

How I Feel Right Now:

(How did this chapter shift your emotions, mindset, or motivation?)

____

____

____

____

How I'll Apply It:

(What action, boundary, or habit will you commit to changing or improving after reading this?)

____

____

____

____

Prayer or Affirmation for Today:

(Write a short prayer or affirmation that aligns with what you're learning and becoming.)

"Discipline your mind, protect your peace, and the crown will follow."
— *Cortlandt Coleman*

"Silence is a source of great strength."

—Lao Tzu

Day 6 — Divine Alignment: When Preparation Meets Purpose

"When you outgrow certain rooms, God will build new ones around your purpose."

My Reflection

When I started purging my circle, it was lonely. I didn't understand why people I loved suddenly couldn't stay in my space.
But looking back now, I see that separation was *protection.*
God had to remove distractions before He could release direction.

And here's the wild part: once I found my focus, the same people who dismissed me suddenly wanted to reconnect, collaborate, and ride the wave.
But I learned that not everyone who wants to be around you is meant to go *with* you. Some people are just spectators to your transformation, not partners in your purpose.

When God started aligning me, He placed me in new environments, networking rooms filled with hungry women in their 20s and beyond, trying to find their voice, their path, and their freedom.
And I'll be real, working with young women isn't easy. Many haven't developed discipline yet. Some still chase validation over vision. But I know that's where my *assignment* lives.

Because sometimes God positions you not to impress, but to *impact.*
To awaken the next generation of Queens before they lose themselves chasing everything that doesn't serve them.
This is how purpose unfolds: one conversation, one connection, one calling at a time.

I've learned that when you walk in your purpose, the money follows the mission. When you pour into others, the overflow always finds its way back to you.

Today's Affirmation

"I am aligned with divine purpose. God connects me with the right people, places, and opportunities that multiply my impact and my income."

Journal Prompt

- Who has God placed in your path during this new season of alignment?

- How can you discern between those meant to *learn from you* and those meant to *grow with you*?

- What doors have opened since you started walking in your purpose rather than under pressure?

Note to Self

When God elevates you, it's never just for you; it's for those who are watching you. Keep walking in purpose, stay disciplined, and remember: the money follows the mission, not the other way around.

Reflections of a Queen

"Pause. Reflect. Realign."

Take a moment to breathe and let today's lesson settle in your spirit.
Use this space to write your thoughts, emotions, or next steps.
There's no right or wrong way to reflect, only honesty and intention.

What I Learned Today:

(What truth stood out the most to you from today's message?)

____

____

____

____

How I Feel Right Now:

(How did this chapter shift your emotions, mindset, or motivation?)

____

____

____

____

How I'll Apply It:

(What action, boundary, or habit will you commit to changing or improving after reading this?)

____

____

____

____

Prayer or Affirmation for Today:

(Write a short prayer or affirmation that aligns with what you're learning and becoming.)

____

____

____

____

"Discipline your mind, protect your peace, and the crown will follow."
— *Cortlandt Coleman*

"God doesn't call the equipped, He equips the called."

— John C. Maxwell

Day 7 — Purpose Over Popularity

"Popularity fades. Purpose multiplies."

My Reflection

I won't lie, there are moments when popularity gets to me.
When I see women in the same industry climbing faster, gaining followers, or getting recognized, it can make me question my progress.
I've had to remind myself: **this race isn't about visibility, it's about value.**

Popularity looks beautiful from the outside: the applause, the attention, the validation.
But I've learned that not every loud platform carries lasting impact.
It's not the crowd that confirms your calling, it's the consistency that does.

There were times I felt overlooked, wondering why others were being chosen first.
But God whispered, *"You're not being hidden. You're being prepared."*
He's shaping my message, sharpening my delivery, and building my foundation so when I step on that stage in front of thousands to preach financial literacy, self-development, and wealth-building, I'll speak from wisdom, not from wounds.

So yes, popularity may tempt me. But instead of letting it discourage me, I've learned to let it **fuel my grind.**
I no longer chase followers, I cultivate community.
I don't need global validation, I crave divine confirmation.
Because when you're walking in purpose, the right people will always find you, and the wrong ones will quietly fade away.

Today's Affirmation

"I am not chasing popularity; I'm chasing purpose. I trust that God's timing will reveal my platform when my preparation is complete."

Journal Prompt

- When was the last time you compared your journey to someone else's? What truth did you learn from that moment?

- How can you redirect envy or doubt into motivation and discipline?

- What would "purpose over popularity" look like for you in your current season?

Note to Self

Keep your head down and your crown up. Your spotlight is coming, not because you chased it, but because you were faithful in the dark. The right people will hear your voice when it's time.

Reflections of a Queen

"Pause. Reflect. Realign."

Take a moment to breathe and let today's lesson settle in your spirit.
Use this space to write your thoughts, emotions, or next steps.
There's no right or wrong way to reflect, only honesty and intention.

What I Learned Today:

(What truth stood out the most to you from today's message?)

____

____

____

____

How I Feel Right Now:

(How did this chapter shift your emotions, mindset, or motivation?)

____

____

____

How I'll Apply It:

(What action, boundary, or habit will you commit to changing or improving after reading this?)

____

____

____

Prayer or Affirmation for Today:

(Write a short prayer or affirmation that aligns with what you're learning and becoming.)

____

____

____

"Discipline your mind, protect your peace, and the crown will follow."
— *Cortlandt Coleman*

"What lies behind us and what lies before us are tiny matters compared to what lies within us."

— Ralph Waldo Emerson

Day 8 — Faith Over Fear: When You're Called to Build Bigger

"Patience isn't sitting still. It's moving with trust, even when the destination isn't visible yet."

My Reflection

One of the hardest lessons I've had to learn is **patience,** not the kind that waits quietly, but the type that works faithfully.
Because truth be told, I've always felt time pressing on me like a clock ticking in the background.

I know time is a limited resource. Once it's gone, it's gone.
And that thought used to stress me every second I wasn't "producing," I felt like I was losing ground.

But then God reminded me: *"You can't rush divine order."*

Mentoring young women taught me the exact truth: they want success fast, results now, purpose on demand. But mastery takes time.
You don't plant a seed and dig it up every day to see if it's growing. You water it, you wait, and you trust what's happening in the dark.

At 39, I see time differently.
If the average woman's life expectancy is around 85 years, that means I've lived nearly half of my book, and now every move I make must count.
That's why I'm building like my life depends on it, because in a way, it does.
There are no off days when you're called to build legacy. But there's also no progress without peace.

So now, I ride on faith, fueled by consistency, guided by patience.

Because I refuse to waste the next 46 years chasing what God already said is mine, I'm just walking it out, one obedient step at a time.

Today's Affirmation

"I trust God's timing. I move with faith, patience, and purpose, never rushing, never retreating, only rising."

Journal Prompt

- What area of your life are you rushing that God is asking you to trust Him with?

- How do you define "productive patience," the kind that builds without burnout?

- How can you model patience and consistency for those you mentor?

Note to Self

You're not running out of time, you're running into divine timing. Keep building, keep believing, and let faith set your pace.

Reflections of a Queen

"Pause. Reflect. Realign."

Take a moment to breathe and let today's lesson settle in your spirit.

Use this space to write your thoughts, emotions, or next steps.

There's no right or wrong way to reflect, only honesty and intention.

What I Learned Today:

(What truth stood out the most to you from today's message?)

____

____

____

____

How I Feel Right Now:

(How did this chapter shift your emotions, mindset, or motivation?)

____

____

____

____

How I'll Apply It:

(What action, boundary, or habit will you commit to changing or improving after reading this?)

____

____

____

____

Prayer or Affirmation for Today:

(Write a short prayer or affirmation that aligns with what you're learning and becoming.)

> *"Discipline your mind, protect your peace, and the crown will follow."*
> — *Cortlandt Coleman*

"The legacy of heroes is the memory of a great name and the inheritance of a great example." — Benjamin Disraeli

Day 9 — Legacy Moves: Building What Outlives You

"Your name is the first business you'll ever own. Honor it, protect it, and make it worth something."

My Reflection

Let's be honest, it's no longer about *us*.

It's about our children, grandchildren, and the generations coming after them.

Every decision we make today plants a seed in tomorrow's soil.

So I ask myself daily:

What do I want my legacy to be built on?

Who am I leaving it to?

And when they speak my name long after I'm gone, what will they remember me by?

That's why I tell my kids and the young adults I mentor:

"Honor your name and move like you're getting paid to use it."

Let that sink in.

Because when you see your name as currency, you start protecting your image, your word, and your reputation differently.

When I was younger, my focus was on fun, meeting guys, hoping for love, and wishing for marriage. But as I grew, I realized how much time we waste chasing temporary attention instead of building permanent value.

Now, every time I step out of my house, I'm representing **my brand, my family, my legacy, my purpose.**

I'm intentional about what I post, what I say, and how I move, because when I'm gone, my *brand* will still speak for me.

I'm building influential leaders in my household, not just children who inherit wealth, but children who understand *why* it was built.

Failure is not a final destination in my home; it's a lesson, a strategy, a test of persistence.

My goal is to leave my kids not just *money*, but **momentum.**

To pass them a business that outlives me, assets that multiply, and a mindset that refuses to go back to struggle.

Because let's be real, generational wealth isn't just about inheritance. It's about information.

It's easier to reach your goals when someone before you has already paved the way. And that's precisely what I'm doing, paving roads my great-grandchildren will never have to crawl through.

Today's Affirmation

"I am building a legacy that will outlive me. My name carries value, purpose, and power that will bless generations to come."

Journal Prompt

- What do you want your children, grandchildren, or community to remember you for?

- How are you actively protecting and building your "name brand" each day?

- What financial or emotional habits do you want to pass down, and which ones stop with you?

Note to Self

You are not just building for today, you are building for eternity. Move like your name is wealth, because one day, it will be.

Reflections of a Queen

"Pause. Reflect. Realign."

Take a moment to breathe and let today's lesson settle in your spirit.
Use this space to write your thoughts, emotions, or next steps.
There's no right or wrong way to reflect, only honesty and intention.

What I Learned Today:

(What truth stood out the most to you from today's message?)

____

____

____

____

How I Feel Right Now:

(How did this chapter shift your emotions, mindset, or motivation?)

____

____

____

____

How I'll Apply It:

(What action, boundary, or habit will you commit to changing or improving after reading this?)

Prayer or Affirmation for Today:

(Write a short prayer or affirmation that aligns with what you're learning and becoming.)

"Discipline your mind, protect your peace, and the crown will follow."
— *Cortlandt Coleman*

"The legacy of heroes is the memory of a great name and the inheritance of a great example." — Benjamin Disraeli

Day 10 — The Power Behind Your Name

"Your name is your first brand, your first promise, and your lifelong signature."

My Reflection

My name is **Cortlandt Coleman,** and no, it's not the most common girl's name. People often pause when they hear it, smile, and say, *"That's beautiful. What's the story behind it?"*

And every time, I smile back and think, *the story isn't finished yet, I'm still writing it.*

My name carries weight.

When I refer someone to a person or business, I make sure that connection is built on **integrity**, because I know my name is attached to it.

If my name is in the room, my reputation is too, and I take that seriously.

That's why I don't give access to everyone.

If I'm vouching for you, it's because your values align with mine: faith, focus, and follow-through.

I don't play about my name, because it's not just about me, it's about every generation that comes after me who will wear it too.

So, I'll ask you the same question I ask my mentees and my own kids:

What's the story behind your name, and are you living up to its beautiful potential?

Your name is the only brand you're born with.

Before the business, before the title, before the followers, your name *is* your identity.

And the way you honor it determines how far it will travel.

Exercise: Define Your Name

Write your full name on paper.

Now, for every letter in your name, write a word that describes **who you are** or **who you're becoming.**

This is how you take ownership of your brand word by word, letter by letter.

Example:

C — Consistent

O — Original

R — Resilient

T — Trustworthy

L — Leader

A — Ambitious

N — Nurturing

D — Disciplined

T — Trailblazer

Do this with intention because every word is a reflection of your future and a declaration of your destiny.

Today's Affirmation

"My name carries power, purpose, and promise. I represent it with integrity, and I'm becoming the woman my name deserves to be attached to."

Journal Prompt

- What emotions or memories come up when you hear your own name?

- Are you protecting your name with the same care you protect your dreams?

- How do you want people to describe your name when you're not in the room?

Note to Self

Your name was given for a reason. Build it. Protect it. Live up to it because one day, it will open doors your presence never could.

Reflections of a Queen

"Pause. Reflect. Realign."

Take a moment to breathe and let today's lesson settle in your spirit.
Use this space to write your thoughts, emotions, or next steps.
There's no right or wrong way to reflect, only honesty and intention.

What I Learned Today:

(What truth stood out the most to you from today's message?)

____

____

____

____

How I Feel Right Now:

(How did this chapter shift your emotions, mindset, or motivation?)

____

____

____

____

How I'll Apply It:

(What action, boundary, or habit will you commit to changing or improving after reading this?)

____

____

____

____

Prayer or Affirmation for Today:

(Write a short prayer or affirmation that aligns with what you're learning and becoming.)

____

____

____

____

"Discipline your mind, protect your peace, and the crown will follow."
— *Cortlandt Coleman*

"Your name is your brand. Your story is your power."

— Simon Sinek

Day 11 — The Assignment of Your Gift

"Your gift will make room for you, but only if you prepare to walk through the door when it opens."

My Reflection

My grit has always been *not knowing*.

I can't stand sitting in a room and not understanding the topic, the language, or the direction of the conversation.

That feeling drives me; it's not insecurity, it's **fuel.**

So, I replaced TV time with *book time.*

While others binge-watch shows, I binge-read wisdom.

There are mornings I wake up and head straight to the bookstore, hungry for knowledge.

And yes, I'll walk out with a stack of books over a hundred dollars deep, shaking my head thinking, *"Girl, what were you thinking?"*

But then I hear that whisper from God:

"This is preparation for what's coming next."

And instantly, it makes sense.

Because every book I open, every paragraph I highlight, every concept I wrestle with, it's all training for my next assignment.

You never know which page holds the answer to your next breakthrough.

That's why I keep feeding my mind and stretching my capacity.

Because one thing I know is that when the opportunity comes, I don't want to be caught saying, *"I don't know."*

So, I'll ask you: are you filling your shelf with books for the future, or are you scrolling social media for validation in the present?

One builds your mind. The other drains your time.

Your gift is God-given. But the **development of it** is on *you.*

Today's Affirmation

"I am sharpening my gift daily. I prepare in private for the purpose that will one day make me public."

Journal Prompt

- What areas of your life make you uncomfortable because you "don't know enough"?

- What are three subjects you could study this month that would strengthen your purpose or business?

- How can you turn your downtime into development time?

Note to Self

Keep feeding your gift. Every book you read, every class you take, every note you study is God preparing you for the rooms you're destined to lead.

Reflections of a Queen

"Pause. Reflect. Realign."

Take a moment to breathe and let today's lesson settle in your spirit.

Use this space to write your thoughts, emotions, or next steps.

There's no right or wrong way to reflect, only honesty and intention.

What I Learned Today:

(What truth stood out the most to you from today's message?)

____

____

____

____

How I Feel Right Now:

(How did this chapter shift your emotions, mindset, or motivation?)

____

____

____

____

How I'll Apply It:

(What action, boundary, or habit will you commit to changing or improving after reading this?)

____

____

____

____

Prayer or Affirmation for Today:

(Write a short prayer or affirmation that aligns with what you're learning and becoming.)

"Discipline your mind, protect your peace, and the crown will follow." — Cortlandt Coleman

"Your talent is God's gift to you; what you do with it is your gift back to God."

— Leo Buscaglia

Day 12 — The Power of Preparation

"Success doesn't start in the morning; it starts the night before."

My Reflection

I used to think I could keep everything in my head: appointments, goals, tasks, deadlines.

I was the woman who said, *"I'll remember."*

But as I got older, I realized the mind may slow down, but the discipline must speed up.

Being ready for anything doesn't just happen; it's a daily decision.

Now, I prepare the night before, plan my schedule, set priorities, and check my intentions.

Preparation gives peace. It keeps my home in order, my business in motion, and my mind focused.

My husband once told me, *"You can't save the world if you're leaving your own tasks undone."*

That hit home. Because it's true, I have a heart to help everyone, but sometimes I was pouring from an unorganized cup.

The key isn't to do less, it's to **do better.**

Balance doesn't mean giving equal time to everything; it means giving the *right* time to the *right* things.

As a mother, wife, and businesswoman, I've learned not to add more to my plate than God gave me grace to carry.

It's okay to say no.

It's okay to pause.

But it's not okay to keep living unprepared.

Preparation is an act of faith, it says, *"God, I believe something big is coming, so I'm getting ready now."*

Today's Affirmation

"I am prepared, disciplined, and balanced. My consistency creates clarity, and my preparation positions me for promotion."

Journal Prompt

- What are three things you could do *tonight* to make tomorrow smoother?

- Where in your life are you overcommitting instead of organizing?

- What system (planner, digital calendar, to-do list) can you use to keep a balance between home, work, and purpose?

Note to Self

Preparation is protection. Stay ready so you don't have to get ready and never let your desire to help others distract you from the order God called you to build first.

Reflections of a Queen

"Pause. Reflect. Realign."

Take a moment to breathe and let today's lesson settle in your spirit.
Use this space to write your thoughts, emotions, or next steps.
There's no right or wrong way to reflect, only honesty and intention.

What I Learned Today:

(What truth stood out the most to you from today's message?)

____

____

____

____

How I Feel Right Now:

(How did this chapter shift your emotions, mindset, or motivation?)

____

____

____

____

How I'll Apply It:

(What action, boundary, or habit will you commit to changing or improving after reading this?)

____

____

____

____

Prayer or Affirmation for Today:

(Write a short prayer or affirmation that aligns with what you're learning and becoming.)

____

____

____

____

"Discipline your mind, protect your peace, and the crown will follow."
— Cortlandt Coleman

"By failing to prepare, you are preparing to fail."

— Benjamin Franklin

Day 13 — Consistency Is the Real Currency

"Consistency will take you where motivation can't."

My Reflection

I used to live my days like the wind wherever it blew; that's where I went.
Some days I was productive; others I was distracted, and my results showed it in my business, my finances, and even my peace.

It took me some time to realize that **consistency is the key to everything bigger.**
Dreams don't fail. We're not gifted; they fail because we stop showing up.
Every goal I've ever reached came from discipline, not desire.

Motivation feels good, but it fades.
Consistency? That's a lifestyle.
It's waking up and doing the work even when you don't feel inspired.
It's building systems instead of excuses.
It's understanding that every small, steady step compounds into something massive over time.

When you look at your bank account, your habits, and your relationships, they all reflect your level of consistency.
If your results are unstable, it's because your effort is inconsistent.

But here's the good news: You can fix that today.
Start small, stay steady, and make your grind predictable even when your circumstances aren't.
Because once you master consistency, *everything else bows to it.*

Today's Affirmation

"I show up for myself daily. My consistency builds confidence, and my discipline attracts destiny."

Journal Prompt

- Where in your life or business are you consistent, and where are you slipping?

- What daily habit could you commit to for the next 30 days that would change your results?

- How can you measure your consistency each week to hold yourself accountable?

Note to Self

Consistency isn't about perfection; it's about persistence. Keep showing up, even when no one's watching. Because the harvest only comes to those who didn't quit planting.

Reflections of a Queen

"Pause. Reflect. Realign."

Take a moment to breathe and let today's lesson settle in your spirit.
Use this space to write your thoughts, emotions, or next steps.
There's no right or wrong way to reflect, only honesty and intention.

What I Learned Today:

(What truth stood out the most to you from today's message?)

____

____

____

How I Feel Right Now:

(How did this chapter shift your emotions, mindset, or motivation?)

____

____

____

How I'll Apply It:

(What action, boundary, or habit will you commit to changing or improving after reading this?)

____

____

____

Prayer or Affirmation for Today:

(Write a short prayer or affirmation that aligns with what you're learning and becoming.)

____

____

____

____

"Discipline your mind, protect your peace, and the crown will follow."— Cortlandt Coleman

"Great things are not done by impulse, but by a series of small things brought together."

— Vincent Van Gogh

Day 14 — The Power of Small Wins

"Big victories are built from small wins repeated consistently."

My Reflection

I used to wait for the *big wins,* the breakthroughs, the bonuses, the life-changing moments.

But life and business taught me that *the big wins don't happen often,* and when you're only motivated by major milestones, you'll burn out before you ever see them.

So I shifted my mindset: small wins became my foundation.

For me, that meant setting **daily goals**, prospecting to at least three people, making at least fifteen follow-up calls, and securing three appointments a day. That was my personal standard.
If I hit it, I sometimes celebrated with a sweet snack or a simple "you did that, girl" moment.

And when I stayed consistent for five days in a row, I rewarded myself with a new dress, a small purse, or a self-care day to recharge.
Those weren't vanity rewards; they were reminders that **discipline deserves celebration.**

But on the days I didn't meet my goals, I didn't reward myself.
Because you can't bless what you didn't build.

This rhythm taught me that **business runs on the law of numbers,** and when you respect your numbers, your income starts to respect you.
I learned to track progress, predict patterns, and push past excuses.

And on those hectic days when I couldn't do it all, my kids would step in, handing out flyers, supporting the mission, watching their mom build something that would one day belong to them.

That's legacy in motion, turning small wins into generational lessons.

Today's Affirmation

"I celebrate small wins as signs of progress. Every call, every connection, every day of effort moves me closer to overflow."

Journal Prompt

- What are three "small wins" you can commit to achieving daily or weekly?

- How can you celebrate your consistency without losing focus?

- Who can you include in your process: children, friends, or team to help you multiply your momentum?

Note to Self

Success isn't built in a day; it's built daily. Track your numbers, trust your grind, and celebrate the small wins that lead to your most significant victories.

Reflections of a Queen

"Pause. Reflect. Realign."

Take a moment to breathe and let today's lesson settle in your spirit.
Use this space to write your thoughts, emotions, or next steps.
There's no right or wrong way to reflect, only honesty and intention.

What I Learned Today:

(What truth stood out the most to you from today's message?)

____

____

____

How I Feel Right Now:

(How did this chapter shift your emotions, mindset, or motivation?)

____

____

____

How I'll Apply It:

(What action, boundary, or habit will you commit to changing or improving after reading this?)

____

____

____

Prayer or Affirmation for Today:

(Write a short prayer or affirmation that aligns with what you're learning and becoming.)

____

____

____

____

"Discipline your mind, protect your peace, and the crown will follow."
— Cortlandt Coleman

"Great things are not done by impulse, but by a series of small things brought together."

— Vincent Van Gogh

Day 15 — The Law of Numbers: Mastering the Grind

"You can't outdream your discipline, and you can't outtalk your numbers."

My Reflection

When I learned the **Law of Numbers**, everything about business started to make sense.

I realized that success isn't magic, it's *math.*

The more people you reach, the more appointments you set. The more appointments you set, the more clients you close. The more clients you close, the more families you impact.

Once I understood that pattern, I stopped guessing and started tracking.

I started following systems that were already working instead of wasting energy trying to create new ones.

Because the truth is, if a system isn't broken, you don't fix it; you **master it.**

As entrepreneurs, we love being creative. We want our own version of everything, our own process, our own style, our own way.

But sometimes, that creative pride slows us down.

You don't have to reinvent what's already proven. You just have to learn how to make it **yours.**

And no, that's not stealing.

It's **cultivating.**

In the corporate world, everyone builds on someone else's framework. Every major company pivots off an existing concept and improves it.

The real question is: *who can deliver it better?*

When I started embracing that truth, my business grew faster, and my confidence grew stronger.

Because I wasn't chasing luck now, I was following **laws.**

And the Law of Numbers doesn't lie.

Track your calls. Track your contacts. Track your closings.

The math will always reveal the mindset.

Today's Affirmation

"I am not reinventing the wheel, I'm refining it. I follow proven systems with my own purpose-driven spin, and the results multiply."

Journal Prompt

- What systems or strategies in your business already work, and how can you strengthen them?

- Where have you been trying to reinvent what's already proven effective?

- What daily or weekly numbers can you start tracking to predict your growth?

Note to Self

Business isn't about copying, it's about cultivating. Learn the laws, trust the math, and stay consistent. The results will always follow the rhythm of your grind.

Reflections of a Queen

"Pause. Reflect. Realign."

Take a moment to breathe and let today's lesson settle in your spirit.

Use this space to write your thoughts, emotions, or next steps.

There's no right or wrong way to reflect, only honesty and intention.

What I Learned Today:

(What truth stood out the most to you from today's message?)

____

____

____

How I Feel Right Now:

(How did this chapter shift your emotions, mindset, or motivation?)

____

____

____

How I'll Apply It:

(What action, boundary, or habit will you commit to changing or improving after reading this?)

____

____

____

Prayer or Affirmation for Today:

(Write a short prayer or affirmation that aligns with what you're learning and becoming.)

____

____

____

____

"Discipline your mind, protect your peace, and the crown will follow."
— *Cortlandt Coleman*

"Don't watch the clock; do what it does. Keep going."

— Sam Levenson

Day 16 — Systems Over Emotion

"Emotions are valid, but systems are vital."

My Reflection

If there's one thing I've learned in business, it's this: **you can't make long-term decisions with short-term emotions.**
It doesn't matter how much you like someone if the business isn't performing; you have to face it with logic, not loyalty.

There were times I let my relationships cloud my judgment.
I stayed quiet when I should've spoken up.
I delayed tough conversations because I didn't want to hurt feelings.
And every time, it costs me in peace, progress, or profit.

Now I know better.
If your business partner isn't performing, that doesn't mean throwing away the relationship; it means having a real conversation.
Sometimes it's not betrayal; it's miscommunication.
And a 20-minute talk can clear the fog that's been holding your business back for months.

You must know when to sit at the **boardroom table**, not the **breakroom table.**
Friendship operates on emotion.
Partnership operates on expectation.

That's why I live by this rule:
"Run your business through systems, not sympathy."
Systems don't lie. They show the truth of who's producing, who's slacking, and where things are breaking down.
If your structure is strong, no emotional storm can shake it.

So, I've learned to separate *business decisions* from *personal feelings*.
Because feelings pass, but systems last.

Today's Affirmation

"I lead with grace, but I manage with structure. My emotions don't control my business, my discipline does."

Journal Prompt

- Have you ever made a business decision based on emotion instead of data or systems? What did you learn?

- What systems (check-ins, accountability trackers, reports) can help keep your business relationships clear and consistent?

- How can you communicate business expectations without damaging personal relationships?

Note to Self

You can care about people and still hold them accountable. Never confuse empathy with excuses. Structure is love, too.

Reflections of a Queen

"Pause. Reflect. Realign."

Take a moment to breathe and let today's lesson settle in your spirit.
Use this space to write your thoughts, emotions, or next steps.
There's no right or wrong way to reflect, only honesty and intention.

What I Learned Today:

(What truth stood out the most to you from today's message?)

____

____

____

____

How I Feel Right Now:

(How did this chapter shift your emotions, mindset, or motivation?)

____

____

____

____

How I'll Apply It:

(What action, boundary, or habit will you commit to changing or improving after reading this?)

____

____

____

____

Prayer or Affirmation for Today:

(Write a short prayer or affirmation that aligns with what you're learning and becoming.)

____

____

____

____

"Discipline your mind, protect your peace, and the crown will follow."
— *Cortlandt Coleman*

"Success is neither magical nor mysterious. Success is the natural consequence of consistently applying basic fundamentals."

—Jim Rohn

Day 17 — Grace in Leadership: Correct Without Crushing

"True leadership isn't about control, it's about cultivation."

My Reflection

When I first started leading people, I thought the goal was perfection.

If someone didn't perform the way I expected, I got frustrated, disappointed, or even discouraged.

But then I learned something powerful: **you can't grow people through pressure alone.**

Leadership takes grace.

It means learning how to *correct without crushing,* to teach without tearing down.

Some people need structure. Others need encouragement.

And the real strength of a leader is knowing the difference.

There were times when my tone was too sharp or my expectations weren't clear.

I had to remind myself that everyone on my team doesn't think like me; some are still learning, still growing, still finding their confidence.

And instead of leading from frustration, I had to learn to lead from *faith.*

That doesn't mean letting people slide or avoiding accountability.

It means holding people to a standard with **grace, not ego.**

I've had to correct people I cared about deeply, team members, friends, even family, but I learned to do it in love.

Because if your correction breaks their confidence, you've lost a builder.

But if your correction lifts their awareness, you've gained a leader.

So now, I check myself before I check others.

I ask, "Am I leading to prove a point or to push them forward?"

That shift changed everything: my team, my culture, and my results.

Today's Affirmation

"I lead with grace and truth. My correction builds confidence, not fear. I'm a leader who grows people, not just profits."

Journal Prompt

- Think of a time you had to correct someone you led. How did you handle it, and what would you do differently now?

- How can you balance compassion with accountability in your leadership?

- What words or approaches help you deliver corrections that uplift instead of discouraging?

Note to Self

Grace in leadership doesn't mean being soft; it means being strategic. Lead with patience, speak with purpose, and always build people, not just results.

Reflections of a Queen

"Pause. Reflect. Realign."

Take a moment to breathe and let today's lesson settle in your spirit.

Use this space to write your thoughts, emotions, or next steps.

There's no right or wrong way to reflect, only honesty and intention.

What I Learned Today:

(What truth stood out the most to you from today's message?)

____

____

____

____

How I Feel Right Now:

(How did this chapter shift your emotions, mindset, or motivation?)

____

____

____

____

How I'll Apply It:

(What action, boundary, or habit will you commit to changing or improving after reading this?)

____

____

____

____

Prayer or Affirmation for Today:

(Write a short prayer or affirmation that aligns with what you're learning and becoming.)

____

____

____

____

"Discipline your mind, protect your peace, and the crown will follow."
— *Cortlandt Coleman*

"Leadership is not about being in charge. It is about taking care of those in your charge."

— Simon Sinek

Day 18 — Energy Is Currency: Protect Your Flow

"You can't pour from an empty spirit; protect your energy like it's money in the bank."

My Reflection

There are days I wake up discouraged when home life, business, and relationships all feel off balance.

Those are the mornings I have to remind myself: *energy is currency.*

Every thought, every emotion, every conversation is a transaction, and not every transaction is profitable.

Sometimes, I've spent energy trying to fix things that weren't mine to fix, rushing to restore relationships, correct situations, or solve problems without checking in with God first.

And every time, I paid for it with exhaustion and frustration.

It's hard pouring into everything at once, family, clients, team, community, without realizing your emotional account is running low.

And when you don't pause to refill, you start responding from emotion instead of wisdom.

That's when mistakes happen. That's when peace slips.

So now I ask myself:

Am I in control of my emotions, or are my emotions controlling me?

Because emotional discipline is spiritual maturity.

When you can handle a bad situation with grace, when you can breathe instead of react, pray instead of panic, that's growth.

That's proof you're mastering yourself before managing others.

Protecting your energy isn't selfish; it's sacred.

You can't build a legacy from burnout.

You can't heal people if you're bleeding inside.

You can't lead effectively if your peace is unstable.

So, before you try to fix everything around you, ask God to fix what's going on *within* you.

Then move accordingly with wisdom, not impulse.

Today's Affirmation

"I protect my peace and my purpose. My emotions are in alignment with my faith, and my energy flows where it's valued, not wasted."

Journal Prompt

- Where in your life do you feel emotionally drained right now, and what's causing it?

- When was the last time you handled a bad situation well? What changed in you that allowed that growth?

- What boundaries do you need to set (or reset) to protect your energy and peace this week?

Note to Self

Your energy is your power. Don't waste it proving, pleasing, or performing. Direct it toward peace, purpose, and prayer; that's where your flow multiplies.

Reflections of a Queen

"Pause. Reflect. Realign."

Take a moment to breathe and let today's lesson settle in your spirit.

Use this space to write your thoughts, emotions, or next steps.

There's no right or wrong way to reflect, only honesty and intention.

What I Learned Today:

(What truth stood out the most to you from today's message?)

____

____

____

____

How I Feel Right Now:

(How did this chapter shift your emotions, mindset, or motivation?)

____

____

____

____

How I'll Apply It:

(What action, boundary, or habit will you commit to changing or improving after reading this?)

____

____

____

____

Prayer or Affirmation for Today:

(Write a short prayer or affirmation that aligns with what you're learning and becoming.)

"Discipline your mind, protect your peace, and the crown will follow."
— *Cortlandt Coleman*

"Energy flows where attention goes."

— Tony Robbins

Day 19 — The Power of Reflection: Don't Just Go Through It, Grow Through It

"Everything you've prayed for has already been planted, but God won't water what you refuse to tend."

My Reflection

One night, I had a dream.

I was walking beside God in the Garden of Eden.

I looked around and asked, *"Lord, why am I here?"*

He said:

"Everything you prayed for has been planted in this garden. Yet, you still haven't watered them."

He continued,

"I gave you a mentor and people who share your vision and mindset, but you don't follow their guidance. You pray for community but isolate yourself from the very people I sent to help you grow."

I stood there silently.

Then he said,

"You keep praying for more when you haven't used what I've already given you. You say you're waiting on Me, but I'm waiting on you. You have the seeds, the tools, the soil, but no action."

And then, with a tone that pierced my spirit, He said:

"When you cry like My Son, bleed like My Son, and surrender like My Son, you'll understand that His death was for humanity's choices, and you have those same choices. But you can't expect change without work."

That dream shook me.

It reminded me that reflection without correction leads to stagnation.

God doesn't repeat instructions; He redirects purpose.

Now I see that prayer without obedience is procrastination dressed in the language of faith.

You can't just pray for fruit; you have to water the garden.

So, I stopped asking God for signs and started acting on His assignments.

And the moment I began to move, the blessings I prayed for began to grow.

Today's Affirmation

"I am watering what God has already planted. I walk in obedience, take action with faith, and grow through every season of my life."

Journal Prompt

- What "seeds" has God already planted in your life that you've been neglecting?

- Who has He sent to mentor or support you that you haven't fully connected with yet?

- What daily actions can you take to start watering what you've been praying for?

Note to Self

God already answered your prayers; they just look like work. Stop asking for new ground when you haven't cultivated the one you're standing on.

Reflections of a Queen

"Pause. Reflect. Realign."

Take a moment to breathe and let today's lesson settle in your spirit.

Use this space to write your thoughts, emotions, or next steps.

There's no right or wrong way to reflect, only honesty and intention.

What I Learned Today:

(What truth stood out the most to you from today's message?)

____

____

____

 How I Feel Right Now:

(How did this chapter shift your emotions, mindset, or motivation?)

____

____

____

How I'll Apply It:

(What action, boundary, or habit will you commit to changing or improving after reading this?)

____

____

____

Prayer or Affirmation for Today:

(Write a short prayer or affirmation that aligns with what you're learning and becoming.)

"Discipline your mind, protect your peace, and the crown will follow."
— *Cortlandt Coleman*

"Follow effective action with quiet reflection. From the quiet reflection will come even more effective action." — Peter Drucker

Day 20 — Faith in Action: Water What You Prayed For

"Faith without follow-through is just wishful thinking."

My Reflection

After that dream of walking with God in the Garden, I woke up different.
I stopped asking and started *acting*.

God had already told me: *"Everything you prayed for has been planted."*
So I decided it was time to start watering.

I got up, picked up the phone, and began prospecting new clients.
I started making my calls, following up with purpose, and closing business.
In just two weeks, I earned $3,000 while still working a full-time job.

Now, that number might not sound big to everyone,
But to me, it was proof that God's promise works when **you do.**

That experience taught me something I'll never forget:
God will meet you at your level of movement.
He wasn't waiting for my perfect plan; he was waiting for my consistent action.
Faith opened the door, but work walked me through it.

Too many of us pray for blessings but never prepare to hold them.
We ask God to increase us, but we never build systems to manage what He sends.
We write vision boards but never write business plans.

Now, I understand that prayer is communication, but **execution** is confirmation.

So, I keep my prayer journal open and my planner ready.
Every goal I write down is my way of saying,

"Lord, I believe in what I asked You for, enough to move toward it."

Today's Affirmation

"My faith moves mountains because my actions match my prayers. I'm watering every seed God has planted with consistency, obedience, and belief."

Journal Prompt

- What prayers have you been speaking but not acting on?

- How can you align your daily habits with what you've been asking God for?

- What has your recent obedience taught you about faith and discipline?

Note to Self

God doesn't bless intentions. He blesses execution. Faith is the blueprint, but work is the builder. Keep watering your garden; the harvest is closer than you think.

Reflections of a Queen

"Pause. Reflect. Realign."

Take a moment to breathe and let today's lesson settle in your spirit.
Use this space to write your thoughts, emotions, or next steps.
There's no right or wrong way to reflect, only honesty and intention.

What I Learned Today:

(What truth stood out the most to you from today's message?)

____

____

____

____

How I Feel Right Now:

(How did this chapter shift your emotions, mindset, or motivation?)

____

____

____

____

How I'll Apply It:

(What action, boundary, or habit will you commit to changing or improving after reading this?)

____

____

____

____

Prayer or Affirmation for Today:

(Write a short prayer or affirmation that aligns with what you're learning and becoming.)

____

____

____

____

"Discipline your mind, protect your peace, and the crown will follow."
— *Cortlandt Coleman*

"*Pray as though everything depended on God. Work as though everything depended on you.*"

— St. Augustine

Day 21 — Harvest Season: Reaping What You've Worked For

"The harvest doesn't come to those who wait; it comes to those who work while they wait."

My Reflection

There's something sacred about finally seeing fruit from the seeds you've sown.
For years, I prayed, planned, cried, and questioned if it was all worth it.
But when I started *watering what I prayed for,* everything began to change.

The same effort that once felt invisible suddenly began producing results: new clients, greater consistency, growing income, and more profound peace.
But the real harvest wasn't just the money.
It was the **proof** that faith and discipline will always produce results when mixed with obedience.

I used to wonder when it would be "my season."
Now I understand that *your season starts the day you get serious.*

God doesn't give fruit to people who won't farm.
He rewards the ones who plant, protect, and persevere through dry days.
He honors the woman who keeps showing up, even when no one claps for her.
Because while others are scrolling and doubting, she's sowing and believing.

Every late night, every sacrifice, every time you chose faith over fear, it mattered.
You didn't just work for money; you worked for mastery.
You didn't just build for yourself; you built for the generations behind you.

Now the harvest is here, not by luck but by *law*.

The law of obedience. The law of numbers. The law of faith in action.

Everything you've planted with integrity is returning with interest.

Today's Affirmation

"I am in my harvest season. I receive every blessing I've worked, prayed, and prepared for. My faith, my consistency, and my obedience are bearing fruit."

Journal Prompt

- What part of your current "harvest" are you most grateful for, spiritual, emotional, or financial?

- What lessons did the planting and waiting seasons teach you that you'll carry forward?

- How can you sustain your harvest without slipping back into old habits or comfort zones?

Note to Self

You are the evidence that God's promises work. Keep sowing, keep stewarding, and keep speaking life, because every seed of faith grows in due season.

Reflections of a Queen

"Pause. Reflect. Realign."

Take a moment to breathe and let today's lesson settle in your spirit.

Use this space to write your thoughts, emotions, or next steps.

There's no right or wrong way to reflect, only honesty and intention.

What I Learned Today:

(What truth stood out the most to you from today's message?)

____

____

____

How I Feel Right Now:

(How did this chapter shift your emotions, mindset, or motivation?)

____

____

____

How I'll Apply It:

(What action, boundary, or habit will you commit to changing or improving after reading this?)

____

____

____

Prayer or Affirmation for Today:

(Write a short prayer or affirmation that aligns with what you're learning and becoming.)

____

____

____

____

"Discipline your mind, protect your peace, and the crown will follow."
— *Cortlandt Coleman*

"You reap what you sow."

— Galatians 6:7

Day 22 — Sustaining the Harvest: Don't Let Comfort Kill Your Calling

"Every season of harvest comes with a test of distraction."

My Reflection

When you finally step into your harvest season, it feels powerful. Doors open, prayers begin to manifest, and momentum builds.
But here's the truth most women won't say out loud: **the enemy doesn't attack when you're empty, he attacks when you're full.**

When your business is moving, your confidence is rising, and your spirit is aligned, distraction will try to creep in through the people closest to you.
Sometimes that distraction comes through the person you share a bed with.

If your partner starts doubting your dream or questioning your focus, don't let that shake you.
You can love them and still stay loyal to your assignment.
I've lived this in my marriage; there were seasons when the enemy used division, discouragement, and doubt to pull me off course.
But the last time, I recognized it for what it was, spiritual warfare, and I rebuked it.
I kept my heart, mind, and soul on God, reminding myself how far He'd already brought me.

A harvest season is an opening you might not get back.
So when that door cracks open, **plant both feet, ten toes down, and run your race.**
Don't get comfortable. Don't slow down to convince anyone to believe in what God already confirmed.

Pray over your husband, your boyfriend, your companion, because when your business is rooted in faith, the enemy will always try to attack your foundation first.

And remember, harvest isn't only about money or success.
It's also about your relationships, your peace, your healing, your spiritual growth.
Sometimes, the blessing is realizing who can't go with you into your next level.
That's not rejection, that's refinement.

Today's Affirmation

"I guard my harvest with prayer, patience, and discernment. I am focused, faithful, and fearless. No distraction will detour my destiny."

Journal Prompt

- Who or what has challenged your focus during this harvest season?

- How can you protect your peace and still lead with love?

- What signs show you when the enemy is trying to use distraction or division in your personal relationships?

Note to Self

Your harvest is holy. Don't argue with doubt; outwork it. Pray over your partner, protect your peace, and stay planted until the season shifts.

Reflections of a Queen

"Pause. Reflect. Realign."

Take a moment to breathe and let today's lesson settle in your spirit.
Use this space to write your thoughts, emotions, or next steps.
There's no right or wrong way to reflect, only honesty and intention.

What I Learned Today:

(What truth stood out the most to you from today's message?)

____

____

____

How I Feel Right Now:

(How did this chapter shift your emotions, mindset, or motivation?)

____

____

____

How I'll Apply It:

(What action, boundary, or habit will you commit to changing or improving after reading this?)

____

____

____

Prayer or Affirmation for Today:

(Write a short prayer or affirmation that aligns with what you're learning and becoming.)

____

____

____

____

"Discipline your mind, protect your peace, and the crown will follow."
— *Cortlandt Coleman*

"Do not pray for an easy life, pray for the strength to endure a difficult one."

— Bruce Lee

Day 23 — Discerning the Attack: When the Enemy Comes for Your Mind and Marriage

"A woman's spirit can sense a storm before the thunder ever hits."

My Reflection

Spiritual warfare doesn't always show up wearing horns; sometimes, it shows up wearing a familiar face.

The enemy won't always attack your money or your business first; sometimes, he starts in your *home*.

When I sense warfare rooted in my husband or my kids, the first thing I do is look at what's feeding their spirit.

What are they watching on TV?

What kind of music or conversations are shaping their energy?

Who are they listening to, and what kind of mindset is being planted through those words?

See, the enemy is sneaky; he uses whatever portal we leave open.

That's why you have to be vigilant about what enters your home.

Every song, show, podcast, or "friend's advice" carries energy.

And when those frequencies don't align with peace, they plant confusion.

As women, God gave us a spiritual warning system, intuition mixed with discernment.

We can feel when something in our household is off long before it entirely unfolds.

Some women ignore it until it builds into destruction.

Others, like me, choose to *nip it in the bud.*

One of the most powerful habits I've built is reading to my husband at night.

Not because he can't read, but because I know, as the provider and protector, his time is stretched thin.

Before bed, I pour into him with self-development, mindset, and scripture.

That's how I cover my household through shared growth, not silence.

And ladies, let me be real for a moment: there is no perfect relationship.

Stop letting social media and love stories lie to you.

Every relationship takes constant work, patience, prayer, and practice.

The couples that last are the ones who *choose each other daily*, even through the tests.

And please, stop letting single people coach you on covenant.

Everybody wants love, but few want to *grow* for it.

A lasting relationship isn't built on perfection; it's built on two people who refuse to give up while they're still growing.

Today's Affirmation

"I am spiritually alert and emotionally grounded. I guard my home, my heart, and my marriage with prayer, discernment, and daily growth."

Journal Prompt

- What outside influences are currently shaping your family's mindset, and do they align with peace or distraction?

- How can you bring spiritual and self-development conversations into your home?

- What signs show you when it's time to pray over your partner instead of arguing with them?

Note to Self

The enemy attacks what's aligned, that's how you know you're in purpose. Stay prayed up, stay alert, and build a home that's unshakable because it's grounded in growth, not perfection.

Reflections of a Queen

"Pause. Reflect. Realign."

Take a moment to breathe and let today's lesson settle in your spirit.

Use this space to write your thoughts, emotions, or next steps.

There's no right or wrong way to reflect, only honesty and intention.

What I Learned Today:

(What truth stood out the most to you from today's message?)

____

____

____

____

How I Feel Right Now:

(How did this chapter shift your emotions, mindset, or motivation?)

____

____

____

____

How I'll Apply It:

(What action, boundary, or habit will you commit to changing or improving after reading this?)

____

____

____

____

Prayer or Affirmation for Today:

(Write a short prayer or affirmation that aligns with what you're learning and becoming.)

____

____

____

____

"Discipline your mind, protect your peace, and the crown will follow."
— *Cortlandt Coleman*

"Be alert and of sober mind. Your enemy the devil prowls around like a roaring lion looking for someone to devour." — 1 Peter 5:8

Day 24 — The Ministry Within Marriage: Building Together Through Faith and Focus

"Teamwork is the rhythm that keeps covenant alive."

My Reflection

There's a reason God created partnership, because purpose was never meant to be carried alone.

The word *TEAM* to me means:

T – Teach
E – Everyone
A – A
M – Mission

A real team knows the mission, and the mission is always *unity*.

When you get married, people say you "become one."
To me, that means becoming one in **spirit, purpose, and divine connection with God.**
Because over time, you start reflecting the person you're with, you think alike, talk alike, even move alike.
That's not a coincidence.
That's spiritual connectivity.
You can tell when two people are truly unified; they don't have to speak to understand each other.
They operate in alignment because their energy is synced.
But alignment doesn't happen by accident; it occurs through accountability and agreement.

That same principle applies to **mentorship.**

When God sends a mentor, He's not sending a replacement for your brain. He's sending *wisdom to fast-track your breakthrough.*

So why pray for guidance, only to reject it when it doesn't fit your comfort zone?

Let's be honest, Queen, if your current way of thinking were enough to reach your next level, you wouldn't be praying for help.

The purpose of a mentor is to *compress time,* shortening the struggle it takes to get to where they already are.

You asked for elevation, but elevation requires humility.

And just like in marriage, when you pray for a spouse but still want to live single, you create confusion.

You ask for partnership but resist accountability.

You ask for leadership but ignore instruction.

Growth demands submission not to a person's control, but to God's process.

Sometimes, the answer isn't doing more; it's finally **listening** and following the plan.

Because success doesn't just come from doing, it comes from doing what's *proven.*

So, whether it's your husband or your mentor, stop fighting structure.

Sometimes, letting someone else lead for a season is the fastest way to learn how to lead well yourself.

Today's Affirmation

"I am a team player in purpose and partnership. I align with wisdom, follow instruction, and move in unity with the people God sent to grow me."

Journal Prompt

- What does "team" mean in your marriage, business, or mentorship?

- Are you truly following the plan your mentor or partner helped you build, or are you rewriting it from comfort?

- Where do you need to release control and let trust lead?

Note to Self

Partnership is the power behind progress. Stop praying for teamwork while playing solo. Teach, listen, align, and move together; that's how missions are won.

Reflections of a Queen

"Pause. Reflect. Realign."

Take a moment to breathe and let today's lesson settle in your spirit.
Use this space to write your thoughts, emotions, or next steps.
There's no right or wrong way to reflect, only honesty and intention.

What I Learned Today:

(What truth stood out the most to you from today's message?)

____

____

____

____

How I Feel Right Now:

(How did this chapter shift your emotions, mindset, or motivation?)

____

____

____

____

How I'll Apply It:

(What action, boundary, or habit will you commit to changing or improving after reading this?)

____

____

____

____

Prayer or Affirmation for Today:

(Write a short prayer or affirmation that aligns with what you're learning and becoming.)

____

____

____

____

"Discipline your mind, protect your peace, and the crown will follow."
— *Cortlandt Coleman*

"A cord of three strands is not quickly broken." — Ecclesiastes 4:12

Day 25 — Submission vs. Surrender: Learning the Difference Between Control and Cooperation

"There's a thin line between love and hate, and an even thinner one between submission and surrender."

My Reflection

For a long time, I struggled with the words *"submission"* and *"surrender.*
Both sounded like giving up, shrinking, or losing control, and as a strong woman, that never sat right with me.

But life and love taught me something deeper: **submission and surrender aren't the same, but they both serve a purpose.**

Submission is *intentional alignment.*
It's saying, "I trust you enough to lead in this moment," whether that's your spouse, your mentor, or God.
It's not weakness, it's wisdom. It's knowing when to stand firm and when to let cooperation move things forward.

Surrender, on the other hand, is *spiritual release.*
It's what happens when you stop fighting what you can't control and let God do what only He can.
It's peace that comes from acceptance, not defeat.

I've learned to pick my battles carefully.
Not every situation deserves my reaction.
Some moments call for submission, quiet strength, stillness, and strategic agreement.

Other moments call for surrender, letting go of what I can't fix and trusting God to handle the rest.

The problem is, too many of us hear those words and think they mean *weakness*. But baby, it takes real strength to stay calm when you could explode. It takes maturity to follow when you could fight. It takes faith to surrender when you can't see the whole picture.

So, let me ask you: what's holding you back from seeing submission and surrender as *spiritual strategies* rather than emotional sacrifices?

Because maybe, just maybe, your next level isn't waiting for another fight, it's waiting for you to flow finally.

Today's Affirmation

"I know when to submit and when to surrender. My peace is my power, and my discernment is my strength."

Journal Prompt

- In what areas of your life are you resisting submission or surrender, and why?

- How can you tell the difference between when God is asking you to *lead* and when He's asking you to *let go*?

- What does healthy submission look like to you in relationships, faith, or leadership?

Note to Self

Submission isn't silence, and surrender isn't weakness. They're both signs that you've mastered the art of balance, knowing when to move and when to let God move for you.

Reflections of a Queen

"Pause. Reflect. Realign."

Take a moment to breathe and let today's lesson settle in your spirit.
Use this space to write your thoughts, emotions, or next steps.
There's no right or wrong way to reflect, only honesty and intention.

What I Learned Today:

(What truth stood out the most to you from today's message?)

____

____

____

____

How I Feel Right Now:

(How did this chapter shift your emotions, mindset, or motivation?)

____

____

____

____

How I'll Apply It:

(What action, boundary, or habit will you commit to changing or improving after reading this?)

____

____

____

____

Prayer or Affirmation for Today:

(Write a short prayer or affirmation that aligns with what you're learning and becoming.)

____

____

____

____

"Discipline your mind, protect your peace, and the crown will follow."
— *Cortlandt Coleman*

"Trust in the Lord with all your heart; do not depend on your own understanding."

— Proverbs 3:5 (NLT)

Day 26 — The Beauty of Becoming: When God Prunes Before He Promotes

"God will prune you privately before He promotes you publicly."

My Reflection

When God starts pruning you, it's not always gentle; it's deep, emotional, and sometimes painful.
But pruning isn't punishment.
It's preparation.

I remember when I went to a women's conference in Las Vegas with over 3,000 women, all of us in the financial service industry. I told my mentor and my roommate that I wanted to see *Tom Brady's rings* in the Hall of Excellence.

They looked at me like I was crazy.
"Tom Brady isn't going to be there," they said.
But my spirit told me, *"Go anyway, you need to see what excellence looks like when you win."*

So we got up early, and when we arrived, I walked through a hall filled with legends: Michael Jordan, Oprah Winfrey, Muhammad Ali, Serena Williams, and the Beatles. Every exhibit told the story of greatness born from grit.
Before we could tour, they handed us an old iPhone with headphones so we could scan the items and hear the story behind each one.

When I got to Tom Brady's section, I froze.
I scanned each of his seven Super Bowl rings, each one more significant than the last. I saw his 6th-round draft card: pick number 199. And as his voice played through the headphones, something shifted in me.

I couldn't move.

My body started tingling.

Tears ran down my face.

At first, I didn't even know why I was crying, but then I heard that still whisper from God:

"The greatness you admire in others is already inside you, but what steps are you taking to bring it out?"

I realized, at that moment, that the most significant battle wasn't the competition around me; it was the doubt *within me.*

Tom Brady's story taught me something: greatness is not about talent; it's about tenacity.

He said his idol was Michael Jordan, and MJ had six rings.

Tom said, *"To be great, you have to beat the great,"* and that's why he stopped at seven.

God used that experience to show me that pruning is the cutting away of comfort. It's the season when He removes distractions, excuses, and even old versions of yourself that can't carry your calling.

And when you feel that sting of pruning, that's when you know promotion is near.

Because **you can't bear fruit without letting Him cut what no longer grows.**

Today's Affirmation

"I embrace my pruning season. Every tear, test, and lesson is shaping me for the greatness God already placed within me."

Journal Prompt

- What area of your life is God pruning right now, what feels uncomfortable, but necessary?

- Who or what might God be removing so you can grow stronger?

- What does "becoming great" look like for you, and what daily steps are you taking to walk in that greatness?

Note to Self

The pain you feel is proof you're growing. Don't resist the pruning; it's the hand of God shaping you for something extraordinary.

Reflections of a Queen

"Pause. Reflect. Realign."

Take a moment to breathe and let today's lesson settle in your spirit.
Use this space to write your thoughts, emotions, or next steps.
There's no right or wrong way to reflect, only honesty and intention.

What I Learned Today:

(What truth stood out the most to you from today's message?)

____

____

____

____

How I Feel Right Now:

(How did this chapter shift your emotions, mindset, or motivation?)

____

____

____

____

How I'll Apply It:

(What action, boundary, or habit will you commit to changing or improving after reading this?)

____

____

____

____

Prayer or Affirmation for Today:

(Write a short prayer or affirmation that aligns with what you're learning and becoming.)

____

____

____

____

"Discipline your mind, protect your peace, and the crown will follow."
— *Cortlandt Coleman*

"He cuts off every branch of mine that doesn't produce fruit, and he prunes the branches that do bear fruit so they will produce even more."

—John 15:2 (NLT)

Day 27 — The Cost of Greatness: When Discipline Becomes Your Superpower

"Discipline is the bridge between your current comfort and your future calling."

My Reflection

Let's be honest, discipline is *complex,* even for the greats.
Everyone sees the success, but few know the sacrifice it takes to get there.

When you're building something bigger than yourself, it costs more than money; it costs *moments.*
The world will point fingers and say,

"Why weren't you at your daughter's volleyball game?"
"Why did you miss your son's boxing match?"
"Why didn't you make it to brunch for Mother's Day?"

And sometimes, those questions sting because you wish you could be everywhere at once.

But discipline means making tough choices that your purpose will thank you for later.
It doesn't mean you don't love your family; it means you're building something that will *one day free them.*
The same people who question your grind now will one day rest in the comfort your discipline created.

I'm not saying sacrifice your family for success, I'm saying **create balance with intention.**
Some seasons require more grind; others demand more grace.
The key is to stay aware of both.

Greatness isn't glamorous; it's lonely, tiring, and often misunderstood.

But those who endure the grind with purpose eventually look back and realize every missed moment built a memory of its own, the story of who they *became*.

The truth is, greatness is expensive, but the reward is generational.

You just have to know when to pause, when to push, and when to *praise God for the progress.*

Today's Affirmation

"My discipline is divine. I balance faith, family, and focus with wisdom and grace. Every sacrifice I make is planting seeds of legacy."

Journal Prompt

- What areas of your life require more discipline right now?

- How can you create more balance between your family and your grind?

- What's one boundary you can set to protect both your goals and your relationships?

Note to Self

Discipline doesn't steal memories; it builds meaning. Keep balancing your grind with gratitude, and one day, your family will thank you for the sacrifices you made today.

Reflections of a Queen

"Pause. Reflect. Realign."

Take a moment to breathe and let today's lesson settle in your spirit.

Use this space to write your thoughts, emotions, or next steps.

There's no right or wrong way to reflect, only honesty and intention.

What I Learned Today:

(What truth stood out the most to you from today's message?)

____

____

____

How I Feel Right Now:

(How did this chapter shift your emotions, mindset, or motivation?)

____

____

____

How I'll Apply It:

(What action, boundary, or habit will you commit to changing or improving after reading this?)

____

____

____

Prayer or Affirmation for Today:

(Write a short prayer or affirmation that aligns with what you're learning and becoming.)

____

____

____

____

"Discipline your mind, protect your peace, and the crown will follow."
— *Cortlandt Coleman*

"We are what we repeatedly do. Excellence, then, is not an act, but a habit."

—Aristotle

Day 28 — The Reward of Rest: Why Even Warriors Need to Pause

"Rest is not weakness, it's recovery."

My Reflection

As I sit here in my **home office**, I can feel the weight and beauty of this moment.
My phone keeps lighting up with text messages from my husband and kids.
"When are you coming out?"
"Are you done yet?"

And truthfully, my heart pulls in both directions.

Because I know how important it is to finish this affirmation journal.
This isn't just another task; it's one of my biggest personal goals.
Completing it means I can finally walk over to my whiteboard and cross it off, a visual reminder that I kept my promise to myself, to God, and to the women I'm writing this for.

But I also know that once this goal is completed, it's time to shift gears to rest, to reconnect, and to be *fully present* with my family this weekend.

Rest doesn't mean laziness; it means reward.
It's a sacred pause to appreciate what your discipline built.
It's spending time with your loved ones, laughing, relaxing, and remembering *why you started in the first place.*

Even the strongest warriors need to lay their swords down sometimes.
You can't fight every battle back-to-back and expect to stay sharp.
Rest isn't quitting, it's sharpening.
Because when you rest right, you return stronger.

So, this weekend, it's **family day**.

I'm closing the laptop, silencing the notifications, and opening my heart.

Because goals are essential, but so are hugs, laughter, and the people who make the grind worth it.

Self-care isn't selfish; it's *stewardship* of your body, mind, and spirit.

When you rest, you honor the work you've done and the God who gave you the strength to do it.

Today's Affirmation

"I honor my need for rest. I pause without guilt, celebrate my progress, and recharge my spirit so I can continue to pour from a full cup."

Journal Prompt

- When was the last time you truly allowed yourself to rest without guilt?

- What does a "perfect rest day" look like for you physically, emotionally, and spiritually?

- Who fills your cup when you take time to step away from the grind?

Note to Self

You deserve the same love, patience, and grace you give to everyone else. Celebrate your small and big wins, then rest, recharge, and rise again.

Reflections of a Queen

"Pause. Reflect. Realign."

Take a moment to breathe and let today's lesson settle in your spirit.

Use this space to write your thoughts, emotions, or next steps.

There's no right or wrong way to reflect, only honesty and intention.

What I Learned Today:

(What truth stood out the most to you from today's message?)

____

____

____

____

How I Feel Right Now:

(How did this chapter shift your emotions, mindset, or motivation?)

____

____

____

____

How I'll Apply It:

(What action, boundary, or habit will you commit to changing or improving after reading this?)

____

____

____

____

Prayer or Affirmation for Today:

(Write a short prayer or affirmation that aligns with what you're learning and becoming.)

"Discipline your mind, protect your peace, and the crown will follow."
— *Cortlandt Coleman*

"Come to me, all of you who are weary and carry heavy burdens, and I will give you rest."

— Matthew 11:28 (NLT)

Day 29 — Crossing the Finish Line: The Power of Completion

"Finishing what you start is the quietest but loudest form of confidence."

My Reflection

There's something sacred about finishing.
It's not just about the applause, it's about the *becoming*.

When I started writing this affirmation journal, I knew it would take more than motivation; it would take **commitment.**
There were long nights, early mornings, and moments when life tried to pull my attention away.
But I refused to quit.

Now here I am in my home office, seeing that whiteboard goal finally gets its checkmark.
It's not just ink on a board; it's proof of follow-through.
It's evidence that when you stay faithful, God finishes what He started *through you.*

Completion carries a power that's hard to explain.
It builds confidence.
It heals old patterns of inconsistency.
It silences doubt and strengthens faith.
And it teaches you that discipline isn't about being perfect, it's about *being persistent.*
Sometimes the greatest reward isn't the outcome, it's realizing who you became in the process.

Because every page, every prayer, and every reflection shaped me into the woman I used to only dream about.

Now I understand finishing is a spiritual act.

When you complete something you once thought was impossible, you honor the part of you that refused to settle.

You prove that faith, focus, and follow-through are a holy combination.

So today, I celebrate completion not just as a writer, but as a woman who kept her word to herself.

This is more than a finished journal.

This is a *chapter of transformation.*

Today's Affirmation

"I finish strong. I honor my word, my work, and my walk with God. Every completion is confirmation that I'm capable, called, and covered."

Journal Prompt

- What project or goal have you been putting off that you need to finish this month?

- How does it feel to keep a promise to yourself?

- What lesson did the process of completion teach you about consistency, courage, or faith?

Note to Self

The finish line isn't the end; it's the beginning of a new level. Every time you complete what you start, heaven celebrates, and hell gets nervous.

Reflections of a Queen

"Pause. Reflect. Realign."

Take a moment to breathe and let today's lesson settle in your spirit.
Use this space to write your thoughts, emotions, or next steps.
There's no right or wrong way to reflect, only honesty and intention.

What I Learned Today:

(What truth stood out the most to you from today's message?)

____

____

____

____

How I Feel Right Now:

(How did this chapter shift your emotions, mindset, or motivation?)

____

____

____

____

How I'll Apply It:

(What action, boundary, or habit will you commit to changing or improving after reading this?)

____

____

____

____

Prayer or Affirmation for Today:

(Write a short prayer or affirmation that aligns with what you're learning and becoming.)

____

____

____

____

"Discipline your mind, protect your peace, and the crown will follow."
— *Cortlandt Coleman*

"I have fought the good fight, I have finished the race, and I have remained faithful." — 2 Timothy 4:7 (NLT)

Day 30 — Becoming Her: Walking Boldly Into Your Next Season

"You are the proof that broken things can still build kingdoms."

My Reflection

Being me hasn't been easy.

It took years of lessons, heartbreak, rebuilding, and grace.

I've walked through things most people only see in movies and survived things nobody should ever experience.

There was a time I was held down in my own kitchen, naked and afraid, with a gun to my head during a home invasion.

And yet… I'm still here.

I still became *her*.

That's why I say don't let your circumstances define your future.

Don't let childhood trauma, broken relationships, or absentee parents dictate your destiny.

You are not what happened to you; you are what *you decide to heal from.*

Becoming *her* means reclaiming your identity, your true self, your divine assignment, your crown.

It means understanding that every scar, every failure, every sleepless night was shaping the woman you were always meant to be.

Queens, hear me:

You are beautiful.

You are powerful.

You are fully capable of walking in elegance and confidence, even when your heart has been through hell.

A Queen carries many crowns: friend, sister, girlfriend, wife, mother, aunt, grandmother, and most importantly, **a child of God.**
She walks with clarity, not confusion.
She speaks with conviction, not fear.
She doesn't shrink to fit the room; she adjusts her crown and shifts the atmosphere.

And when a Queen's season changes, she doesn't mourn the old one; she raises her hand high, waves goodbye with gratitude, and walks boldly into her next.
Because she knows that *every ending is just God preparing the stage for her next beginning.*

So today, I say this: **I became her.**
Not because life was kind to me, but because God was.
I became her through grace, through fire, through faith, and now I stand as living proof that you can too.

Today's Affirmation

"I am healed, whole, and walking in purpose. My past built my power. My faith crowns my future."

Journal Prompt

- Who is "Her" to you, the woman you've become through trials, growth, and grace?

- What parts of your past have made you stronger, wiser, or more compassionate?

- How will you carry your crown into this next season of purpose and peace?

Note to Self

Queens don't quit, they evolve. You didn't just survive your story; you rewrote it. Hold your head high, fix your crown, and walk into your next season like you already won, because you did.

Reflections of a Queen

"Pause. Reflect. Realign."

Take a moment to breathe and let today's lesson settle in your spirit. Use this space to write freely, your thoughts, emotions, or next steps. There's no right or wrong way to reflect, only honesty and intention.

What I Learned Today:

(What truth stood out the most to you from today's message?)

____

____

____

____

How I Feel Right Now:

(How did this chapter shift your emotions, mindset, or motivation?)

____

____

____

____

How I'll Apply It:

(What action, boundary, or habit will you commit to changing or improving after reading this?)

____

____

____

____

Prayer or Affirmation for Today:

(Write a short prayer or affirmation that aligns with what you're learning and becoming.)

____

____

____

____

"Discipline your mind, protect your peace, and the crown will follow."
— *Cortlandt Coleman*

"And when the Great Shepherd appears, you will receive a crown of never-ending glory and honor."

— 1 Peter 5:4 (NLT)

Closing Message: The Final Crown

"Becoming Her wasn't just a journey; it was a rebirth."

To every woman who picked up this journal,
Who read these words, reflected, cried, wrote, and healed, this is for you.

You've walked through 30 days of self-discovery, pruning, restoration, and power. You've faced your truth, confronted your past, and planted new seeds for your future.
You've proven that *Queens are built in silence, refined through storms, and revealed through faith.*

I wrote this journal not as a perfect woman, but as a *becoming* woman.
One who has fallen, fought, and risen again.
I've known pain, deep, dark pain, but I've also known the God who turns pain into purpose.

This is my story, my testimony, and my reminder to you:
You are not behind. You are not broken.
You are *becoming*.

Every day you choose faith over fear, forgiveness over bitterness, and discipline over doubt, you're building your legacy.
You're teaching your daughters strength, your sons' wisdom, and your community resilience.

Never forget your crown isn't given, it's *earned through grace.*
Fix it daily. Guard it fiercely. Wear it proudly.

And when you look in the mirror, say this out loud:

" I am her, the healed, the whole, the worthy, the chosen.
I am walking in my divine assignment,
And I will not apologize for shining."

With Love & Legacy,

Cortlandt Coleman
Founder, *Queens of Capital Collective*
Creator of the Queens of Capital Collective 90-day Planner

"A Queen doesn't just rise, she teaches others how to."

I AM… The Becoming, The Becoming, The Becoming.

1. I am the healed version of the little girl who once wondered if she was enough — today, I KNOW I am more than enough.

2. I am becoming the woman I prayed for with discipline, intention, and divine alignment.

3. I walk boldly into every next season prepared, powerful, and protected.

4. I am a woman of success. Success flows to me because I am built for it.

5. I know exactly what I want, and I move with clarity, confidence, and conviction toward it.

6. I have a definite chief aim. I SPEAK it, I ACT on it, and I ATTRACT it through faith and repetition.

7. I trust my voice, my gut, and my God together; they create my path.

8. My past shaped me, but it does not define me; I define me.

9. I release anyone and anything that disrupts my peace or delays my destiny.

10. I am a magnet for abundance, wealth, wisdom, and wellness that flow to me effortlessly.

11. I move in silence and let my results testify louder than my words.

12. I honor the calling on my life. I walk in rooms like God sent me, because He did.

13. I am consistent, disciplined, and committed to my evolution.

14. I attract the right mentors, partners, resources, and opportunities to advance to the next level.

15. I operate not from fear, but from power, strategy, and purpose.

16. I am chosen, favored, and strengthened for every battle and every blessing.

17. I am building a legacy. My name carries weight, honor, and future generational wealth.

18. I am powerful beyond measure; nothing about me is accidental.

19. I am HER healed, elevated, focused, and fearlessly walking in divine alignment.

20. I rise boldly, beautifully, and unapologetically into my next season, the season God prepared with my name on it.

A Queen Reflections

9 798218 890216